Great Western 'through and through' – but, in fact, built at Swindon in 1949 after the nationalisation of Britain's railways – No 7020 *Gloucester Castle* draws admiring glances from the strollers in Sydney Gardens. Having called at Bath station, No 7020 – less than a year old when photographed here by Ivo – presents a stirring sight as she gathers speed with a London-bound express.

STEAM AROUND BATH

Maximum effort – S&D class 7F No 53806 climbs through Lyncombe Vale, Bath, with the 11.20 am down freight. The banker, at the rear of the train, is just emerging from Devonshire Tunnel.

19 March 1955

STEAM
AROUND
BATH

Mike Arlett
&
Ivo Peters B.E.M.

INTRODUCTION

I still recall my surprise when I first browsed through just some of Ivo's many albums of railway photographs, for I had expected to see only pictures of his beloved 'Somerset & Dorset' line! But I was soon to learn that, ever since Ivo began to photograph trains in 1925, his interests have extended far beyond the Mendip Hills. As a result, Ivo's pictures present a superb record of many of this country's railways, including industrial and narrow-gauge systems. Nearly 500 such photographs, including some taken on childhood visits to Germany, were later to be included in Ivo's book *Somewhere Along the Line*, published in 1976.

Several years ago, I mentioned to Ivo my hope that, one day, he might consider submitting for publication a selection of his photographs taken in and around Bath, portraying not just the Somerset & Dorset line but all of the railways, including those lines which had, perhaps, received less than adequate coverage elsewhere. I well remember Ivo turning to his desk and handing to me a loose-leaf binder which contained a detailed synopsis for a photographic album provisionally entitled 'Steaming around Somerset and Surrounding Counties'. Ivo had obviously already given considerable thought to the very book which I – and I suspect many others – hoped would be published!

But this was not to be, for in 1981, Ivo suffered a sudden and serious illness and thereafter concentrated what effort he could on completing his quartet of picture albums portraying the Somerset & Dorset in the 1950's and the 1960's. Thankfully, not only did Ivo complete that classic work, but made a partial recovery of health to the extent that I, and many other friends, can still enjoy the pleasure of visiting him at his home in Bath.

Last year, I suggested to Ivo that he might wish to give some further thought to a book based on the synopsis which he had previously shown to me. Ivo's response was to the effect that whilst he was no longer able to undertake such a project single-handed, he would provide the photographs, if I would, in turn, write the captions and supporting text. Well, I have taken up the challenge, knowing of course that whatever I write, most people will choose to buy the book because of Ivo's photos! But if, hopefully, the captions do add to your enjoyment of the pictures, then I shall be more than pleased.

The format of this book has been based upon Ivo's previous publications – and deals, in turn, with each of the railways around Bath in 'journey order'. Earlier, I referred to Ivo's book *Somewhere Along the Line*. Despite a marked lack of publicity, the book soon sold out and, ironically, many enthusiasts only learned of its publication long after it was out of print. As a result, the book has since become something of a collector's item and Ivo frequently receives enquiries as to where a copy may be obtained! With such requests in mind, the opportunity has been taken to include in the following pages a number of relevant photographs from *Somewhere Along the Line*. The large majority of pictures, however, are previously unpublished, and have been selected by Ivo to portray the wide variety of motive power which worked around Bath. Indeed, the local railway enthusiast was often spoilt for choice, as witness the locomotives of the former Great Western, Southern and LMS, together in later years, with the BR 'Standards' and the more occasional 'interloper'. All could be seen – and will be recalled – in *Steam around Bath*.

Mike Arlett   Trowbridge, 1987

ACKNOWLEDGEMENTS

We wish to thank Derek Mercer and Peter Skelton, both of whom have been to considerable trouble to obtain the best possible prints from Ivo's negatives, a few of which are now more than 60 years old! Our thanks are also extended to Duncan Harper for drawing the maps reproduced within this book, and to Mrs Alex Summers for typing – and often retyping – the captions and supporting text. As with all of Ivo's books, Mrs Angela O'Shea has played a most important role with her help in the choice of prints and their final arrangement. Photographs taken, other than by Ivo, are individually credited.

Published 1987
Millstream Books
7 Orange Grove
Bath
BA1 1LP

ISBN 0948975075

Photographs (except where otherwise credited) © Ivo Peters
Text © M. J. Arlett 1987.

Set and printed in Great Britain by Netherwood Dalton & Co., Bradley Mills, Huddersfield, Yorks.

In the 1930's, Southern Railway engines operated some of the through services over the GWR from Portsmouth to Bristol and back, passing through Bath. A Drummond 4-4-0 Class D15 No 472 – built for the L&SWR in 1912 – prepares to resume her return journey from Bath, with a Bristol to Portsmouth train.   *1932*

The fascination of steam – An up express, hauled by a 'King', passes Saltford at high speed; the coaches rocking and swaying on track that was still suffering from the deterioration of maintenance during and after the Second World War.

CONTENTS

PART 1   BATH TO BRISTOL (G.W.R.)

BATH SPA STATION

The Great Western station at Bath did not acquire the courtesy title 'Bath Spa' until the early years of nationalisation. The station, as originally built, possessed an overall roof, but in 1897 this feature was demolished and the station rebuilt.

1 The focus of attention for these two locospotters is diverted away from No 6818 *Hardwick Grange* towards the incoming train – the 9.15am from Paddington, headed by No 7020 *Gloucester Castle*. On the right is a wagon turntable, by which access was gained to the 'stub' sidings accommodated within the very limited space available at the east end of the station. Such features have long since disappeared and the down platform today extends right up to the river bridge.

4 April 1959

2 Another once-prominent feature at Bath station – again now removed – the elevated signal box, perched high above the canopy of the down platform. But all eyes here are upon ex-Great Western 4-4-0 *City of Truro* which has just been restored to working order and, looking absolutely superb, is standing in the middle road at Bath prior to working back to Swindon on a running-in turn. The figure standing at the foot of the platform ramp is the well-known railway photographer, Kenneth Leach, who is about to be invited 'on board' for the return run.

25 March 1957

THE SHUNTING COMPANIONS

3 No 7014 *Caerhays Castle* runs into the station with the 11.15am Weston Super Mare to Paddington express, passing on the right, the stable occupied by Prince, the Bath shunting horse. For many years Prince, who can be seen 'on shed', was used to shunt wagons in and out of the short sidings at both ends of the station.   *19 March 1949*

4 The form of motive power more generally associated with shunting, ex-GW 0-6-0 pannier tank No 7749 (the Bath pilot engine) stands in the middle road between duties. Driver Cannings is in charge of No 7749.
6 June 1949

RUNNING-IN TURNS AT BATH

A series of photographs showing the variety, and the development, of the Great Western 4-6-0's. All were photographed at Bath station on running-in turns, following overhaul at Swindon.

5 'Saint' class No 2927 *Saint Patrick*, a 2-cylinder 4-6-0 built at Swindon in 1907. Was this, perhaps, her final overhaul prior to scrapping?

27 July 1950

6 'Star' class No 4031 *Queen Mary*, a 4-cylinder 4-6-0, was the first in her class to be fitted from new with a super-heater when built in October 1910. She was withdrawn from service 18 months after Ivo photographed her. *4 February 1950*

7 'Castle' class No 7014 *Caerhays Castle* built in 1949 to a design originating from 1923. As seen here, she has just been fitted with a double-chimney, 4-row superheater and a Davis & Metcalfe lubricator.

28 February 1959

8 'King' class No 6000 *King George V* built in 1927, the doyenne and best-known member of a famous class. When Ivo photographed her at Bath, No 6000 was adorned in the unfamiliar, and short-lived, bright blue livery bestowed upon all express passenger locomotives soon after nationalisation in 1948.

22 June 1949

9 Brand new: BR 'Britannia' Pacific No 70020 *Mercury* pauses at Bath a few days after allocation to the Western Region. The 'Britannias' were built at Crewe; Nos 70017 to 70029 all being allocated new to the Western Region in 1951. *18 August 1951*

WELCOME

AND

FAREWELL

10 An elderly lady nearing her final days: 'Bulldog' class 4-4-0 No 3438 can still attract the attention of young and old alike as she awaits the 'right away' with a parcels train bound for Bristol. *20 August 1949*

TWERTON TUNNEL

Two miles out of Bath station, the Great Western line passed through Twerton tunnel to emerge beyond the western outskirts of the city. Here a signalbox controlled two sidings, one on either side of the line, but little used in later years.

11 A view taken from the signalbox, with No 5025 *Chirk Castle* heading westwards with a down express against the backcloth of Carr's Wood. *28 May 1949*

12 No 6019 *King Henry V* has just emerged from Twerton tunnel, and accelerates the 4.15pm Paddington to Plymouth express past the signalbox in the early evening sunshine. *29 May 1950*

13 This picture of 2-6-0 No 6378 heading towards Bristol with a class **K** freight train offers a closer view of the western portal of Twerton tunnel which, as at the east end, was built to this high arched and castellated design, complete with twin turrets.

29 August 1961

14 By the early 1960's both sidings at Twerton had been lifted and the signalbox closed. Rebuilt SR Bulleid Pacific No 34046 *Braunton* passes the disused box with an excursion from Poole to Cardiff.

12 August 1962

15 A down local pulls away, hauled by No 6974 *Bryngwyn Hall*, and passes the signalbox in which Ivo spent so many happy hours. *4 October 1950*

SALTFORD

Saltford station was to Ivo, in his childhood days, what Midford was to become to me. Here, in the early 1920's Ivo gained the friendship of the station master Mr Redwood, and the signalman Mr Potter, both of whom widened Ivo's early knowledge of railway operation. This, in turn, encouraged the development of what was to become a lifetime interest – railway photography.

16 Resplendent in Great Western livery, having been converted to oil-firing and renumbered, No 3955 *Haberford Hall* pauses at Saltford with an up local on a running-in turn. Ivo was, however, more concerned for the ganger standing in the down line who was, apparently, blissfully unaware of a fast-approaching Bristol express! *1947*

17 At many a country station, the highlight of the day was often the arrival of the local 'pick-up' goods train. Saltford was no exception, and on this occasion the train was worked by a 'Bulldog' class 4-4-0. The footbridge is worthy of study, complete with GWR monograms; that on the near (down) side partially obscured by the 'Parcels Office & Cloakroom' signboard.

1930

18 A busy scene as a 'Hall' class 4-6-0 approaches the station with an up train, passing a 2-6-2T setting off with a local bound for Bristol, Temple Meads.

1948

19 A 'Saint' class 4-6-0 passes through the station at high speed with a down express. The small goods yard at Saltford included a hand-crane and a covered shed – the latter, a modest structure clad with galvanised iron.

1931

20 On the 22 August 1953, 2-6-2T No 5527 burst a steam pipe in her cab whilst approaching Saltford with a down local train. After some delay, an 0-6-0PT No 7718 was sent out from Bristol and, having removed 5527 to the goods yard, took the local forward into Bristol. No 5527, her crew having escaped uninjured, awaits the attention of the local fire brigade. Ivo's son Julian, who was sitting on the lineside fence, was a spectator to the incident.

SALTFORD IN THE EVENING

21 A Hawksworth 'County' – a class instantly recognizable by the flat-topped wheel splashers and 'straight' nameplates. No 1014 *County of Glamorgan* was but three years old when Ivo photographed her drawing away from Saltford with an evening up local.

8 June 1949

22 No 4708, one of the impressive Churchward mixed-traffic 2-8-0's, has just returned to traffic following overhaul at Swindon, and looks immaculate in plain black livery, setting off towards Bristol with the evening running-in turn – the 5.00pm local from Swindon. *29 May 1956*

NEARING KEYNSHAM
        23 On a very cold day, a 'King' in full cry approaches Keynsham with the down 'Bristolian'.
16 March 1959

24 Another 'ex-works' Churchward 2-8-0 No 4707, this time leaving Keynsham during a heavy rain-storm. The main interest lies, perhaps, with the leading coach, still with clerestory roof, and in service as a stores van. The vehicle is of a somewhat grander origin – having formed part of the Royal train provided by the GWR for Queen Victoria way back in 1897!   *6 April 1951*

25 Two famous 'old ladies'. Caledonian Single No 123 built in 1886 – she took part in the races to Edinburgh in 1888 – and Great Western 4-4-0 No 3440 *City of Truro*. Both engines had been on exhibition at Swindon, in conjunction with the naming ceremony of No 92220 *Evening Star*, the last steam locomotive built by British Railways. Ivo photographed Nos 123 and 3440 approaching Keynsham, en route to Bristol.

25 March 1960

26 The driver's view! A down express, hauled by an ex-GW 'Hall' is framed by the windscreen of Ivo's Bentley, parked in the goods yard at Keynsham. For the technically-minded, Ivo's 'fun-shot' was focused on 60ft and taken at 1.500th at f11, using Ilford HP3 film, developed in Promicrol.

17 February 1958

KEYNSHAM AND SOMERDALE

27 No 4082 *Windsor Castle* pauses at Keynsham & Somerdale station with an up train. The footbridge makes an interesting comparison with that at Saltford and featured in picture 17, reflecting, perhaps, the greater importance of Keynsham station. *24 June 1949*

28 No 6920 *Barningham Hall* runs into the station with an up local. The signals on the left had been pulled off for a down train, the tail of which can be seen disappearing towards Bristol
11 August 1949

In the 1920's the firm of J. S. Fry & Sons erected a large factory near Keynsham for the production of their famous chocolate and cocoa goods. The Company held a competition to select a name for the new complex – the winning title being 'Somerdale'. In 1925 the GWR, aware perhaps of the considerable traffic potential, renamed Keynsham station 'Keynsham & Somerdale'. The factory was served by a private railway system complete with Sentinel locomotive, and linked to the GWR at Keynsham station.

29 0-6-0PT No 7782, is about to pull out of Fry's with loaded vans, passing through the factory gates and across a public road to gain access to the main line at the east end of the station. *24 April 1964*

30 Rebuilt SR Pacific No 34053 *Sir Keith Park* heads the up 'Pines Express' past Keynsham West signal box. The 'Pines' had been rerouted between Poole and Yate to run via Wimborne, Salisbury and Bristol, as the result of a landslip on the Somerset & Dorset line at Midford. The siding leading to Fry's factory can be seen to the left. *7 December 1960*

FOX'S WOOD
WATER TROUGHS

During the 1890's, water troughs were installed at Goring, in Berkshire, and at Fox's Wood between Keynsham and Bristol. These enabled traffic to run non-stop between Paddington and Exeter, and – via the Severn Tunnel – between London and Newport. In later years, when the West of England traffic ran via Westbury, and London to South Wales trains via the Badminton line, the troughs at Fox's Wood were used less intensively.

31 Above: 'Castle' class No 5057 *Earl Waldegrave* passes over the troughs and heads eastwards with the 1.50pm Bristol to Paddington. *30 April 1960*

32 Later in the afternoon, No 5387 'over-indulges', with inevitable results! The firemen can just be seen working hard to lift the tender pick-up scoop clear of the water in the trough. *30 April 1960*

ST. ANNE'S PARK

33 St. Anne's Park, the last station before reaching Bristol, Temple Meads. No 5035 *Coity Castle* emerges from Fox's Wood No 2 Tunnel – sometimes known as St. Anne's Tunnel – with the 9.05am ex-Paddington. *23 February 1950*

34 No 6900 *Abney Hall* heaves a long freight train out of Bristol East Depot, and gains the up main line immediately to the west of St. Anne's Park station. Originally this had been the site of the Fox's Wood No 1 Tunnel, but in 1889 works to create a new marshalling yard involved opening out and widening the 330 yard tunnel to form the deep, vertical-sided rock cutting discernible in the background.

23 February 1950

BRISTOL, TEMPLE MEADS

Despite losing some through traffic from London to the West Country following the completion of the direct route via Westbury and Castle Cary in 1906, Bristol was to remain one of the most important and busy rail centres in Britain. The origins of Temple Meads station were the separate termini of the Great Western and the Bristol & Exeter railways. The stations were adjacent but lay at right-angles to one another and in 1845 the systems were linked by a curved connecting line. Later, following the arrival of the Midland Railway at Bristol, the station was further developed, jointly by the GW and Midland companies. In the early 1930's the station was again extended and partially rebuilt and, following completion in 1935, outwardly remained little changed until the closure, in 1966, of the original Brunel terminus, which had been extended eastwards and, since the 1930's, used by LMS traffic.

Three scenes which show Temple Meads station in 1931 immediately prior to the rebuilding of the joint station.

37 LMS compound 4-4-0 No 1079 propels a train of empty stock towards the Midland carriage sidings, east of Temple Meads. The compound had brought in her train from the north, which terminated at Bristol.

38 GWR 'Saint' class 4-6-0 No 2954 *Tockenham Court* prepares to set off from the south end of the station with a westbound local.

39 Empty stock is brought into the station by a GW 2-6-0, piloting a 2-6-2T past one of the signalboxes which were soon to be made redundant as part of the 1930's modernisation scheme.

Opposite:
35 The south end: a familiar setting which Ivo utilised to portray the restored *City of Truro* pulling away with a special excursion to South Devon.
19 May 1957

36 The north end: GW Mogul No 6384 emerges from the gloom of the overall roof on one of the through lines between platforms 7 (left) and 9 (right), with a train of empty stock. *24 April 1960*

TEMPLE MEADS —
JOINT STATION FOR
THE GWR AND LMS

40 Returning to the south end of the station – ex-LMS 'Jubilee' class 4-6-0 No 45552 *Silver Jubilee* has brought the Home Counties Railway Society 'Mendip Rail Tour' from London to Bristol. Here she is seen propelling the train back into platform 2.   *6 October 1963*

41 Ivo selected this photograph to emphasize the previous 'joint' ownership of the station. An ex-Great Western 2-6-0 No 5384 with a down parcels train stands abreast an ex-Midland Railway 0-6-0 class 4F No 43953, the crew of which can be seen sitting on the track in front of their engine.
10 September 1949

42 GWR 'Dean Goods' 0-6-0 No 2445 eases her train over the pointwork with a westbound express (!) bound for Weston
Super Mare.

10 September 1949

43 On the same day Ivo photographed another of the 'Dean Goods' No 2537, standing in the station at the head of a local train –
the fireman busy on the tender, trimming coal forward.

44 On parade and awaiting their next duties are (left to right) No 7033 *Hartlebury Castle*, No 6986 *Rydal Hall*, and No 1009 *County of Carmarthen*.
16 August 1959

BRISTOL, BATH ROAD SHED

45 An interesting comparison – this photograph, taken 34 years earlier, also features a GW 'County'. But, of course, this is one of the Churchward 4-4-0's of 1904 lineage. Also seen on shed, a 'Star' class 4-6-0 and, alongside, a 'Bulldog' class 4-4-0.
September 1925

When Ivo visited Bath Road Shed on 16 August 1959, he was able to photograph No 7033 *Hartlebury Castle* being prepared for duty. This engine – built in 1950 – had only recently been fitted with a double chimney. Yet within another 3½ years, after a total of just 12½ years in service, she would be condemned and cut up. What a sad waste.

46 No 7033 *Hartlebury Castle* receiving attention at the coaling stage . . .

47 . . . and being turned.

48 A general view of the shed on a cold but fine winter's afternoon: the occupants include 0-4-2T No 1454, 4-6-0 No 5019 *Treago Castle* and a class 633XX 2-6-0.

17 February 1957

49 Another view of the line-up seen in picture 44 – this is a personal favourite which portrays so poignantly the unique atmosphere of a main line running shed. On the extreme right, a BR 'interloper' has sneaked into what otherwise could be very much a 'Great Western' scene.

16 August 1959

INTERESTING VISITORS

50 'A rose between two thorns' – the old Bath Road steam shed has been replaced by a modern diesel depot but plays host on an 'Open Day', to preserved steam locomotives – ex-LMS Pacific No 46201 *Princess Elizabeth* and, in the background, 0-6-0PT No 1638. The privately preserved *Princess Elizabeth* was on a visit from her home base at Ashchurch whilst the ex-GW pannier was en route from Tyseley to the Dart Valley Railway. *21 October 1967*

51 Following display at Bristol, Caledonian Single No 123 and GW No 3440 *City of Truro* prepare to set off for Cardiff, where, again, they were on exhibition to the public.
1 April 1960

ST. PHILIP'S MARSH SHED, BRISTOL

Whereas, primarily, Bath Road served as the depot for servicing and running repairs to motive power employed on passenger traffic, the large depot at St. Philip's Marsh was very much the domain of the heavy freight, mixed-traffic and shunting engines.

53 Another Sunday morning line-up comprising Nos 4655, 2205, 3604, 3731 (displaying a 'Not to be moved' board), 7783, a class 36XX, 6671, 6601.

16 August 1959

52 Inside one of the roundhouses at 'The Marsh' – an impressive array of motive power assembled around the turntable, including (left to right) two BR class 9F 2-10-0's, an ex-LMS 8F 2-8-0, two WD 2-8-0's, another BR 9F, and an ex-GW 'Grange'.

16 August 1959

54 Steam super-power – two of the BR 'Class Nines' – Nos 92204 and 92222. *16 August 1959*

55 There were few more impressive engines – especially when viewed from ground level – than the Churchward mixed-traffic 2-8-0 class 47XX. Those based at St. Philip's Marsh were very much 'birds of the night' – often employed on the night-time express perishables traffic between Bristol and London.

17 February 1957

56 In November 1962, Mr Don Gronow, the shedmaster in charge of Bath Road and St. Philip's Marsh depots, invited Ivo – in the company of his old friend Harold Morris, the Bath Green Park shedmaster – to Bristol to see No 1365, the last remaining member of the 1361 class 0-6-0ST still in use. On their arrival at 'The Marsh', No 1365 had been put away inside the shed, but Mr Gronow promptly arranged for her to be brought out and run to and fro for Ivo to film. Ivo recalled how Mr Gronow then turned to Harold Morris and said 'We really have no use for her at Bristol, Harold, would you like to have her at Bath?' 'Go on Harold, say Yes' whispered Ivo! But sadly, Harold Morris had to decline the offer as there was no suitable work for her at Bath. *8 November 1962*

57 Two ex-GWR 2-8-0's Nos 3803 and 2859, a GW 2-6-0, and WD 2-8-0 No 90179 stand on the coal road. *17 February 1957*

58 'Castle' class No 5054 *Earl of Ducie* had been selected to work the final leg of an Ian Allan special run to commemorate the 60th anniversary of *City of Truro's* exploit down Wellington Bank in 1904. No 7032 *Denbigh Castle* was selected as the standby engine for the anniversary run. *7 May 1964*

59 When members of the Bath Railway Society visited the St. Philip's Marsh motive power depot in early 1957, I doubt whether anyone expected to find a locomotive still bearing the legend 'G.W.R.' some nine years after the demise of the 'old Company' following the formation of British Railways in 1948. But some 'eagle eye' must have spotted something under the layers of grime collected by 0-4-2T No 5813 – and much rubbing revealed again the once-familiar initials. *17 February 1957*

PART 2
BRISTOL TO YATE (LMS)

The route of the Midland Railway, from Bristol to Gloucester, Birmingham and the North, parted company with the Great Western line half a mile to the east of Temple Meads station. Passing the LMS locomotive depot at Barrow Road, and the junction leading to the little known MR terminus at St. Philip's – used until 1951 for some of the local services to Mangotsfield and Bath – the railway climbed north-eastwards out of the City, through the suburbs of Fishponds and Staple Hill.

BARROW ROAD SHED

60 This is, without doubt, one of Ivo's finest photographs – and a personal favourite – the bright shafts of early evening sunlight pierce the gloom of Barrow Road shed and fall upon a line-up of locomotives stabled around the turntable at the end of their day's work.

17 February 1957

61 Amongst the other engines on shed, that same evening, was the diminutive ex-Lancashire & Yorkshire 'Pug' 0-4-0ST No 51202 which, in earlier years, also saw service on the Somerset & Dorset line at Radstock, when she was employed shunting traffic from the local collieries.

17 February 1957

62 Standing outside the shed – two 4-6-0's, 'Black Five' No 44851 and 'Jubilee' class 6P No 45662 *Kempanfelt*, together with a class 5MT 2-6-0 Horwich 'Crab' No 42890.

15 June 1958

63 Locospotters delight – or frustration? Just how long a wait will be necessary before the nearest locomotives move, revealing the numbers of those hidden behind?! The main running lines climb past the motive power depot and under the road bridge (complete with locospotters!) towards Lawrence Hill Junction. *26 July 1959*

64 The view outside the entrance to the shed with a Great Western 2-6-0 'interloper' in the foreground. In the centre, 'Black Five' No 44965 receives last-minute attention prior to coming off shed and reversing down to Temple Meads station. *26 July 1959*

65 Another interesting line-up, including two 4-6-0's, No 44962 and 45651 *Shovell* and a 'Jinty' 0-6-0 tank.   *19 May 1957*

66 The Barrow Road mechanical coaling plant with BR class 5 No 73031 being coaled.   *26 July 1959*

FISHPONDS

The worst of the climb out of Bristol was over on reaching Fishponds, the station which once served as the starting point for a local service to the Clifton Down Line which diverged from the main Midland route into Bristol at Kingswood Junction, ¾ of a mile west of Fishponds station.

67 'The Cornishman', Penzance to Wolverhampton, train which ran via the Midland line between Bristol and Yate, tops the long climb. The train, headed by GW 'Castle' class 4-6-0, No 5045 *Earl of Dudley*. . . .

68 . . . . has been banked from Barrow Road by LMS Ivatt 2-6-2T No 41240, which drops away from the rear of the train approaching Fishponds station. Here, the Ivatt tank will reverse back over the crossover onto the down line, and return to Barrow Road.   *7 April 1958*

STAPLE HILL

69 Stanier class 5 No 44806 passes through Staple Hill station with a North of England express.

6 August 1949

70 Midland compound 4-4-0 No 41039, drifts out of Staple Hill tunnel and slows to pause at the station with a Gloucester to Bristol stopping train. Today, you are more likely to see a bicycle emerging from the tunnel! After closure of the line, the tunnel was lost to use by infill works but has recently been re-excavated and now forms a part of the Bristol-Bath cycle route. *6 August 1949*

71 With the turntable at Bath temporarily out of action, no less than five locomotives – assembled to form a 'train of engines' – were using the triangular junction at Mangotsfield to turn. Having run out from Bath tender first, the engines are seen here setting off forwards through Mangotsfield station towards the North Junction, where they will again reverse (see picture 78).   *7 April 1953*

MANGOTSFIELD

The 10 mile branch line to Bath, opened by the Midland Railway in August 1869, was provided with two connections with the main line at Mangotsfield – one facing north towards Gloucester, the other towards Bristol. This resulted in the formation of a triangular layout, and the original station at Mangotsfield, close to the new North Junction, was closed and replaced by a new station at the junction nearer Bristol where platforms served the main line and the new route to Bath.

72 Signalman Chilcott on duty in Mangotsfield Station signalbox.
7 April 1953

73 Ex-LMS 'Jubilee' No 45660 *Rooke* passes over the points at the approach to Mangotsfield station with the 12.45pm ex-Bristol. The engine is resplendent in new green livery and had been used a few days earlier on a special train calling at Castle Bromwich in connection with the British Industries Fair.

13 May 1950

74 The down 'Cornishman' heads towards Mangotsfield station behind 'Castle' class No 5045 *Earl of Dudley*, obviously a regular performer on this duty in the late spring of 1958 (see also picture 67).

3 May 1958

75 'The Devonian', another named express which ran over the Midland line between Yate and Bristol, Temple Meads, rounds the curve at Mangotsfield North Junction, hauled by class 3P No 40728, piloting 'Black Five' No 44857.

6 August 1949

MANGOTSFIELD

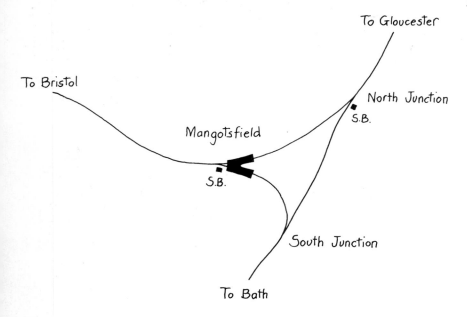

To Gloucester

To Bristol

North Junction

Mangotsfield

S.B.

S.B.

South Junction

To Bath

76 LMS compound No 41074 on a down express, is about to bear left onto the Bath line at Mangotsfield North Junction passing, on the right of the picture, the site of the original station which was closed upon the opening of the branch line to Bath in 1869.

6 August 1949

77 Caprotti class 5 No 44743, running between the South and North Junctions at Mangotsfield, with the up 'Pines Express'.   *3 May 1958*

78 The 'train' of light engines, last featured in picture 71, have run up to Mangotsfield North Junction, where they again reversed to return, tender-first, towards Bath. The locomotives approaching the South Junction are – Stanier 'Black Five' No 44848 (nearest camera), S&D class 7F No 53805, SR Bulleid Pacific No 34042 *Dorchester,* and a pair of class 4F 0-6-0's Nos 43939 and 44146.   *7 April 1953*

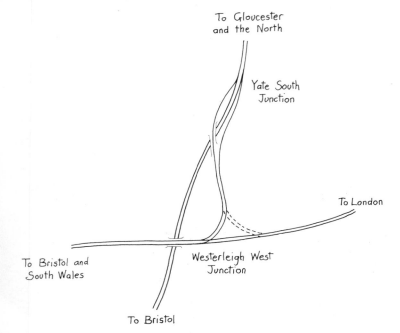

To Gloucester
and the North

Yate South
Junction

To London

To Bristol and
South Wales

Westerleigh West
Junction

To Bristol

79 'A stroke of good luck?' – well, to be honest this picture is not quite what it might seem. Ivo planned this composite picture, photographing the two trains some 5 minutes apart, and if you look carefully, you can see the join. The WR express is heading westwards; the Midland 4F northwards towards Yate. *3 May 1958*

WESTERLEIGH

Some 3¼ miles north of Mangotsfield station, the main line passed by the large goods yards at Westerleigh where much of the Midland's freight traffic to and from Bristol, Bath and the North was marshalled. North, beyond these yards, the Midland line passed under the Great Western main line from Swindon to Bristol and – via the Severn Tunnel – to South Wales. The two lines were linked near Westerleigh by a connection which diverged from the GW line at Westerleigh West Junction and headed northwards. On the approach to the Midland route, the up and down lines forming the connecting spur diverged, the up line crossing the Midland lines by way of a flyover, to connect at Yate South Junction. At various periods between 1903 and 1950 there had been a further connecting loop (shown dotted on the accompanying sketch plan) with the GWR line, providing a junction in the east direction.

80 BR class 5 No 73054, in charge of a freight, heads down the Midland line south of Yate, and passes under the bridge carrying the up line from the GW. *5 March 1961*

81 The up 'Devonian', hauled by two ex-LMS 4-6-0's; class 5 No 45265 pilots 'Jubilee' class 6P No 45677 *Beatty.*   *4 August 1958*

82 A grimy GW mixed-traffic 2-6-0, No 7308, with a down train takes the connecting line between the Midland route at Yate South Junction and the GW at Westerleigh West Junction.   *5 March 1961*

83 Another Churchward Mogul, No 6338, approaches the flyover with an empty coal train.   *18 March 1962*

84 'Britannia' Pacific No 70053, originally named *Moray Firth*, heads the 11.10am (SO) Ilfracombe to Wolverhampton, and is just about to pass under the flyover near Yate. *24 July 1965*

YATE

85 No 5975 *Winslow Hall* passes through Yate station with a down ballast train. *31 March 1963*

86 Earlier in the day, Ivo had photographed this locomotive emerging from Wickwar Tunnel with a down freight train. Unsure whether the destination would be Bristol or Bath, Ivo wisely 'stayed put' and was rewarded, later in the day with this opportunity to photograph the visitor, ER class B1 No 61167 returning north, 'light engine'. *23 July 1961*

NORTHBOUND FROM YATE

— AN INTERESTING VARIETY OF LOCOMOTIVES

87 'Patriot' class 4-6-0 No 45504 *Royal Signals* is seen at the same location, north of Yate, with the 5.00pm Bristol to York train. *13 May 1961*

88 Until the Second World War, the train shed remained fully glazed, including the vertical infill to the open end of the arched roof as seen in this view taken in 1932. This shows the up 'Pines Express' after arrival from Bournemouth. Ex-Midland class 2P 4-4-0 No 518 having backed into the station and coupled onto the train, waits for the carriage doors to be closed before setting off northwards. *July 1932*

PART 3:
BATH TO MANGOTSFIELD (LMS)

THE MIDLAND STATION AT BATH

The Midland Railway opened the 10 mile branch from the main line at Mangotsfield to Bath on 4 August 1869. The terminus, not fully completed until the following May, comprised an elegant frontage building and an iron and glazed train shed. Officially the station was titled just 'Bath', but prior to nationalisation most people knew it as 'Queen Square', a courtesy title which appears to have originated with Bradshaw. In 1951, however, British Railways introduced the more geographically appropriate title for which the station is now perhaps better remembered – 'Bath, Green Park'.

89 Resting in the middle road, ex-Midland Johnson 0-4-4T, No 1391 stands coupled to a Midland clerestory coach. Some of the original Johnson features have been replaced upon the rebuilding of the engine with a Belpaire firebox, closed dome and Ross pop safety valves. *July 1932*

90 Stanier 2-6-2T No 40174, only recently repainted in early BR livery, runs into the station with a local train from Bristol, passing, on the right, the Bonded Warehouse.

26 March 1949

91 In April 1950, the commercial control of the Midland line south-west of Selly Oak (Birmingham) to Bristol and Bath passed to the Western Region as part of the revision of regional boundaries by British Railways. Soon afterwards, some of the local services between Bristol, Mangotsfield and Bath began to be worked by 'Western' motive power, including the GW diesel railcars. Ex-GWR 2-6-2T No 5523 sets off from Green Park, crossing the River Avon with the 6.18pm local to Bristol, Temple Meads.

28 June 1954

92 For several weeks during 1952, the 10.00am Bath to Bristol train was double-headed on Saturday in order to work a Bristol-based engine back to her home shed. Here, the train sets off from Bath, passing the Midland engine shed, behind Ivatt 2-6-2T No 41240 and 2-6-0 No 43012.

7 June 1952

SETTING OFF FROM BATH

93 Compound 4-4-0 No 41078 presents a more graceful sight as she departs with an up express bound for Birmingham and the north.

9 August 1952

'ROYAL SCOTS' LEAVING BATH FOR THE NORTH

94 In the 1950's, a 'Royal Scot' class 4-6-0 was a rare visitor to Bath. Ivo photographed No 46122 *Royal Ulster Rifleman* heading back northwards with the up 'Pines Express'.
12 September 1953

95 No 46106 *Gordon Highlander* departs with the 10.05am Bournemouth to Derby. This 'Scot' was instantly recognizable from the other members of the class, having been fitted with straight-sided BR pattern smoke deflector plates.
24 June 1961

96 Horwich 'Crab' No 42857 has taken over the 10.05am (SO) Bournemouth to Nottingham and Cleethorpes, and gathers speed past the motive-power depot. *16 August 1952*

EX-LMS MOTIVE POWER VARIETY

97 With both 'boards off' for the main line, Stanier 'Jubilee' class 4-6-0 No 45725 *Repulse* heads towards Bath Junction with an up express. *29 May 1960*

INTERESTING VISITORS

It is, perhaps, somewhat ironic that the closer came the decision to divert through traffic away from the Somerset & Dorset line, the greater the variety of motive power working into Bath, to which could be added the more occasional 'interloper'.

98 Ex-LNER class B1 No 61167 sets off for the north with the 11.12am (SO) Bournemouth to Sheffield. *18 June 1960*

99 In September 1962, the Ian Allan organisation ran a rail tour over the S&D behind No 53808. At Bath, ex-GW No 4932 *Hatherton Hall* took over for the run to Bristol on the return journey back to London. *22 September 1962*

THE MIDLAND SHED AT BATH

The original Midland Railway engine shed was erected in 1869. Although relatively small in size, having only two roads, it was a solid structure built in stone. Apart from removal of the doors towards the end of the 1940's, the shed remained little changed over the years.

100 Winter Serenity: Class 2P 4-4-0's, No 40634 and, still with LMS number, No 568, together with class 3F 0-6-0 No 43583, pose behind the turntable.

4 February 1950

101 Summer Saturday: Organized chaos! – An interesting lineup with, left to right, Stanier 2-6-2T No 41242, 0-6-0 No 44096, large-boilered S&D 2-8-0 No 53808, 'Black Five' No 44776, and 'Jubilee' No 45572 *Eire*. No 53808 has been restored to working condition by the S&DR Trust, whilst examples of all the other four classes of locomotives featured in Ivo's photograph have also been preserved.

6 June 1953

MORE RARE VISITORS
FROM THE NORTH

102 'Britannia' No 70034 *Thomas Hardy* had arrived with a down parcels train, and later returned north 'light engine'.
1 May 1965

103 An ex-LNWR Bowen-Cooke 0-8-0 No 48927, from Nuneaton, rests outside the S&D shed at dusk, having brought a special train of phosphate into Bath.
14 January 1956

104 Eastern Region class B1 4-6-0 No 61143.
12 February 1964

105 Class 2P No 40700 and BR class 5 No 73049 run in off the S&D line with the 9.55am (SO) Bournemouth West to Leeds, which has been given precedence over 'Jubilee' No 45643 *Rodney* held with a down train on the Midland line from Mangotsfield. *30 June 1956*

BATH JUNCTION

Half a mile west of Green Park station, the S&D joined the Midland line into Bath.

106 One of Bath's Stanier 0-4-4T's, No 41902, passes Bath Junction with a local service from Bath to Bristol, St. Philip's. *28 May 1949*

A belated departure

107 The engine due to take the relief to the up 'Pines' northwards from Bath has failed! 'Jubilee' No 45682 *Trafalgar* has been hastily despatched from Barrow Road shed, Bristol, to fill the gap. Even so, the train is more than an hour late setting off from Bath, past Bath Junction. On the left, No 53804 waits patiently hoping that perhaps later in the afternoon she might finally be given the opportunity of setting off with the 12.35pm freight!   *20 September 1952*

BATH GAS WORKS

108 Situated on the north side of the Midland line at Bath Junction, the Bath Gas Works was served by its own private rail system. To carry out shunting duties the Works maintained two small saddle tanks – on the left, Avonside No 1978 built in 1928, and behind, the even more diminutive Peckett No 1267 built in 1912.   *21 March 1959*

109 'Jubilee' 4-6-0 No 45725 *Repulse* is working hard, passing through New-bridge, some two miles out of Bath with the up 'Pines Express'. *14 May 1949*

HEADING AWAY FROM BATH

Running westwards from Bath Junc-tion, the Midland line passed through the station serving the suburbs of Weston before emerging into the open countryside near Newbridge.

110 At the same location, but some 17 years earlier, ex-MR Johnson 0-4-4T No 1309 passes by at a more sedate speed with a local train bound for Bristol. The engine is still in original condition with Salter valves on the dome, and a round-topped firebox. *Summer 1932*

111 During the same lineside visit, Ivo also photographed this local goods train hauled by a class 3F 0-6-0. *Summer 1932*

PASSING NEWTON MEADOWS

For a mile or two beyond the western outskirts of Bath, the Midland and Great Western lines ran parallel across the Newton meadows before diverging away from one another when nearing the village of Saltford.

112 Passing by the meadows, the 6.25pm freight from Bath to Avonmouth is drawn by BR class 9F 2-10-0 No 92226.   *13 June 1964*

113 Stanier class 2P 0-4-4T No 1900, the doyenne of the class built in November 1932 saunters by with a Bath to Bristol local. Still in LMS livery, she was one of four of the class (Nos 1900/2/3/4) allocated to Bath between December 1946 and 1949. On a trial over the S&D with a lightweight local, one of these engines found the gradients far from her liking. As a result, all four were relegated to station duties at Bath, and working local passenger traffic to Bristol. All were transferred away from Bath in October 1949, but two moving only as far as Bristol.   *10 September 1949*

114 On New Year's Day, Stanier class 8F 2-8-0 No 48694 simmers away her time beside the woods near Kelston, whilst waiting for further track panels to be unloaded for Sunday relaying works on the Midland line. *1 January 1956*

RUNNING BELOW KELSTON WOODS

115 S & D class 7F 2-8-0 No 53807, skirts the woods with the 6.25pm freight from Bath, which will run to Avonmouth via Kingswood Junction and the Clifton Extension Railway. *8 June 1964*

116 Stanier 0-4-4T No 41903, only recently repainted in lined black livery and displaying the legend 'British Railways' on her side tanks, hurrying by with the evening 'Postal' which must make connection at Mangotsfield with the Midland Region 'Up Postal'. Perhaps this is the justification for the 'express train' headlamp code! *8 June 1949*

STANIER & JOHNSON 0-4-4 TANKS AT KELSTON

117 A Johnson 0-4-4T runs towards Kelston station with a Bristol to Bath local. Ivo photographed the train from the long footpath which led up from the roadway and followed the lineside across the river to the station. *1931*

KELSTON

Kelston station, 4¼ miles from Bath, was one of the earliest of the post-nationalisation casualties in the area covered by this book – the station closing to traffic on 1 January 1949. Primarily, the station served the village of Saltford rather than Kelston which was some distance away. The station could only be approached on foot, intending passengers having to walk some distance from the nearest road along a path running parallel to the line.

118 The 7.10pm 'Postal' from Bath again, this time hauled by class 2P 0-4-4T No 41904, passes the derelict platform at Kelston.
15 July 1949

119 Stanier 0-4-4T No 1900 approaches the disused station with a local from Bath to Bristol.   *6 July 1949*

120 Class 3F 0-6-0 No 43464 ambles past the closed station at Kelston with a down goods bound for the Midland Road Yard at Bath.

6 July 1949

121 Nine days later, the same service was in the hands of No 43373, passing one of Kelston's former signals, from which the arm has been removed. The iron fence to the side of the line protected passengers using the footpath which ran parallel on the down side of the track, and formerly served as the access to the station.

15 July 1949

Towards the end of the 1940's, whereas local passenger traffic was handled by the 0-4-4 tanks, most freight trains were still hauled by either class 3F or 4F 0-6-0's. Both of Ivo's photographs reproduced here depict the rebuilds of Johnson's class 2 engines originally built between 1888 and 1902.

122 Bridge 21, between Kelston and Bitton, was a photographic location chosen by Ivo in pre- and post-war years. In the upper scene, compound 4-4-0 No 1028 is working across from Bath to Bristol with a two-coach local.

Summer 1948

NORTH-WEST OF KELSTON

123 The same location in the early 1930's with unusual motive power – a Johnson 0-4-4T, piloted by a Midland Class 2P 4-4-0 No 526. The latter had no doubt been attached to the train at Bath to avoid a separate light engine working to Barrow Road shed.

Summer 1932

124 In the latter era of the line – BR 2-6-2T No 82004 passes by in charge of a Bath to Bristol train.　　*2 March 1963*

125 S & D class 7F No 53808 nears Bitton with a heavy goods train from Bath to Westerleigh sidings. By the time this book is published No 53808 will again be steaming hard on the West Somerset Railway between Minehead and Bishop's Lydeard.　　*2 March 1963*

BITTON

Bitton station, 6¼ miles from Bath, is now the headquarters of the Bitton Railway Company and, despite many obstacles, substantial progress continues to be made towards the aim to recreate the former glories of the old Midland line. The station has been fully restored and trackwork relayed whilst 'Open Days' attract increasing numbers of the public.

126 LMS 2-6-2T No 40174, crossing the road bridge just south of the station, is framed between two of Bitton's fine MR wooden signals – on the left, the 'down starter' and on the right, the 'up home'.   *11 June 1949*

127 Horwich 'Crab' 2-6-0 No 42822 displays a well-remembered reporting number '220', as she heads the down 'Pines Express' past a scene rich in Midland Railway history – much of which has been recreated in recent years as restoration work at Bitton proceeds.   *11 June 1949*

128 'Black Five' 4-6-0 No 44883 sweeps past the goods yard with a down express. A sister engine, No 45379 is today one of the growing number of locomotives and rolling stock undergoing restoration in the old goods yard and shed at Bitton.

7 August 1950

129 'Black Eight' 2-8-0 No 48463 trundles through the station and past the signalbox with a freight from Bath. The Midland Railway pattern signalbox was demolished following closure of the line, but an almost identical replacement, formerly serving at Painswick Road Crossing box at Gloucester, has been purchased and re-erected at Bitton. *19 May 1964*

BETWEEN BITTON
AND MANGOTSFIELD

130 Class 4F 0-6-0 No 4561 struggles towards Mangotsfield with an early morning freight from Bath. Earlier in the week Ivo had been told that this freight was being worked by one of the S&D 2-8-0's. So, rising at the crack of dawn on the following Saturday, he set off from home to arrive at the lineside soon after 7.00am. But his efforts were on this occasion to be in vain, for the working had reverted to the usual motive power – a class 4F 0-6-0. *Early(!) 1947*

131 This view was taken at Mangotsfield South Junction looking towards Bath. The signal in the background has been pulled off for a Bath to Bristol train which Ivo was 'praying' would not appear and lose him the opportunity of another photograph of the 'train of engines' seen earlier and described with pictures 71 and 78. Here, having turned via the Mangotsfield triangle, they are heading back to Bath, tender-first. *7 April 1953*

132 A view of the junction of the line from Bath and the main ex-Midland line into Bristol. GW 4-6-0 No 5026 *Criccieth Castle* drifts around the curve over the junction points and will pass the main line platforms with the up 'Cornishman'. *29 March 1958*

MANGOTSFIELD

133 Latter-day motive power for a Bristol, Temple Meads to Bath, Green Park local – a BR class 3 2-6-2T runs into Mangotsfield. (From a colour transparency – courtesy Mrs. Angela O'Shea) *17 October 1965*

BATH GREEN PARK

PART 4
BATH TO SHEPTON MALLET
(S&DJR)

134 Although its origins lay with the Midland Railway Company, 'Green Park' will always be remembered best as the northern terminus for the Somerset & Dorset line, whose trains joined the Midland line at Bath Junction, ½ mile west of the station at Bath.

On a dull, cold, Spring day, class 2P 4-4-0 No 568, sets off with a Bournemouth train whilst, on the left, Stanier 0-4-4T No 41902 prepares to leave with a local to Bristol, St Philip's. At this date, some years were still to pass before the Midland station at Bath was to acquire the suffix 'Green Park'.
16 April 1949

135 Ex-S&D class 3F No 3228 has piloted a 4F 0-6-0 into Bath with an up express from Bournemouth. The train has just departed northwards leaving the two engines to reverse out of the station. Note the fashions of the early 1930's, particularly the hats – one of which bears a remarkable similarity in shape to the class 3F's steam dome! *August 1932*

136 This photograph is now becoming quite well-known, but it has to be included – being the very first of Ivo's 'S&D' pictures, taken on his birthday. The rebuilt Johnson 4-4-0, in the distinctive Prussian blue livery of the S&D, is about to leave with a train for Bournemouth.
29 July 1925

137 A pair of 0-6-0 class 4F locomotives – Nos 44561 (ex-S&D No 61) and 44235 – at rest after running in with a heavy up express. This picture pleased Ivo, in that it was unusual to be able to obtain this shot – more often than not the view towards the buffer stops was obstructed by coaching stock stabled in the middle road. *14 July 1951*

138 Ex-LMS class 2P 4-4-0 No 40697 rumbles over the bridge spanning the River Avon, with the 6.50am local from Bournemouth.
5 March 1955

BATH – ARRIVALS AND DEPARTURES
Two pictures which illustrate the wide range of motive power to be seen at Bath in the post-nationalisation era.

139 BR class 9F 2-10-0 No 92212 has taken over the 7.35am (SO) from Nottingham, and sets off with the train for Bournemouth. Having used the northern platform at the station, the train is about to cross over onto the up main line to Bath Junction.
24 June 1961

140 A unique line-up. Three S&D class 7F 2-8-0's standing outside the S&D shed: No 53806 (from the series built in 1925, and still retaining a large-diameter boiler); No 53802 (from the original series built in 1914); and No 53810 (1925 series, but reboilered). This proved to be the one and only occasion that Ivo succeeded in photographing all three variants of the S&D class 7F locomotives in one picture.

19 March 1955.

THE S&D SHED
AT BATH

141 Another interesting line-up photographed a quarter of a century earlier. Ex-MR Johnson 2-4-0 No 157 – built in 1876, less than two years after the arrival of the S&D at Bath. Behind No 157 are an LMS class 2P 4-4-0 and a 3F 0-6-0T.

1932

142 Horwich 'Crab' 2-6-0 No 42897 runs in off the S&D single-line section from Midford with an up express.

28 May 1949

BATH JUNCTION

143 Class 2P No 40601 and 4F No 44139 start the arduous climb towards Combe Down Tunnel with the 7.43am (SO) Birmingham to Bournemouth West. The fireman of the 4F 0-6-0 can be seen retrieving the single-line tablet from the mechanical catcher affixed to the tender.

17 September 1949

144 A pair of class 2P 4-4-0's head the down 'Pines Express' around the long sweeping curve on the early part of the climb out of Bath passing, on the right, Bellotts Road. The train is about to cross over the Great Western Bath to Bristol main line.

1932

145 In the early evening, class 2P No 40697 and large-boilered S&D class 7F No 53807 sweep down the bank past the site of the old brickworks at the lower end of Dartmouth Avenue. This was the first Saturday on which the class 7F 2-8-0's were rostered for use on express passenger trains over the S&D line. Two were used, 53807 as seen in this picture, and 53805 which appears in picture 146.

5 August 1950

146 Class 2P No 40698 and S&D class 7F No 53805 climb the 1 in 50 bank out of Bath, and head towards Devonshire Tunnel with the 7.33am (SO) Nottingham to Bournemouth West. *5 August 1950*

DEVONSHIRE TUNNEL

147 On a sunny Spring day, 7F 2-8-0 No 13801 bursts out of Devonshire Tunnel and into Lyncombe Vale with a down freight. The engine is still in LMS livery, and is yet to be renumbered by the newly created Railway Executive. *30 April 1949*

HORSECOMBE VALE – MIDFORD

When Ivo and I first decided to produce *Steam Around Bath* we agreed that he would be responsible for the final choice of photographs, whilst I would undertake the preparation of the supporting captions. When it came to this part of our book – featuring the Somerset & Dorset – I was more than pleased with our arrangement. For just how do you select 35 pictures from a choice of more than 3,000? One early decision agreed was, that on reaching Midford, we would use just one picture, for as Ivo pointed out, this – a favourite location of ours – has received more than adequate coverage with the recent publication of my book *The Somerset & Dorset at Midford*, which contains over 100 photographs, many of which were generously supplied by Ivo

From the very large choice available, Ivo finally selected the picture above – taken at Tucking Mill, a favourite location, with the impressive 8-arch viaduct set against the wooded slopes of the beautiful Horsecombe Vale with – as a backcloth – the southern rampart of Combe Down, from which the S&D emerged after tunnelling for more than a mile. Ivo recounted to me how, sadly, it was no longer possible to photograph from this superb location after 1955, when the trees in the foreground had grown higher and obscured the parapet of the viaduct.

The train featured in Ivo's photograph is the down 'Pines Express', hauled by 2P 4-4-0 No 40634 – built for the S&DJR in 1928 – and SR Bulleid Pacific No 34040 *Crewkerne*. The southern portal of Combe Down Tunnel can be seen in the background.   *24 April 1954*

149 The Ivatt class 4MT 2-6-0's – referred to by S&D enginemen as 'Doodlebugs' – made their first appearance on the S&D in 1949, and soon gained a reputation as 'bad steamers'. It must have come as some surprise, therefore, to see No 43012 heading northwards from Wellow unassisted with a train of ten coaches! As Ivo suspected, however, he later learnt that No 43012 had received assistance up the southern slopes of the Mendips from Evercreech Junction, and over the summit at Masbury, to Binegar. *20 August 1949*

WELLOW

150 In late April, British summertime having just begun, Ivo was able to photograph the progress of the 7.05pm Bath to Bournemouth southwards as far as Binegar. The attraction, of course, was the motive power – one of the splendid ex-L&SWR class T9 4-4-0's, No 30706, deputising for a failed BR class 4. Here, as the evening shadows lengthen, the 'Greyhound' is seen arriving at Wellow. *26 April 1958*

NEAR STONEY LITTLETON

CLIMBING AWAY FROM RADSTOCK

151 The tranquility of the beautiful countryside around Stoney Littleton, between Radstock and Wellow, is interrupted by a pair of class 4F 0-6-0's Nos 44535 and 44424, as they swing through the curves with a Bournemouth to Leeds express.   *29 July 1954*

152 S&D class 7F No 53809 climbs away from Radstock, passing the 'down advanced starting' signal, with the 5.00pm freight from Bath. A stop had just been made at Radstock station, to enable a 'Jinty' 0-6-0T to couple up and provide rear-end assistance for the 7½ mile climb to Masbury Summit. On the right is the single-line ex-GW North Somerset branch, which features in Part 8 of this book.   *8 May 1954*

MIDSOMER NORTON

Ivo recently showed me a booklet entitled *More Memories*, by Gwen Malcolm, which includes some recollections of Mrs Malcolm's early travels over the S&D from her home near Midsomer Norton. One story, which delighted Ivo, related how the family laundry – sent each week by rail to the laundry at Wells – had been returned and left on the platform to await collection from the station at Midsomer Norton. Shortly afterwards, a heavy goods train passed through, the 'banker' showering the station with sparks and red hot cinders, some of which fell upon the laundry basket. A few minutes later, the signalman noticed a wisp of smoke rising from the basket. He hurried down from his box, and promptly extinguished the fire with the contents of the station watering can – which unfortunately contained a rich mixture of 'manure water'. Those articles of clothing which had escaped the effects of the hot cinders were ruined by the liquid manure!

I think that it may well have been this story which influenced Ivo's choice of photographs.

153 (Above) Big-boilered S&D class 7F No 13808 climbing hard towards the station with a heavy freight. . . .

154 (Right) . . . . 'banked', at the rear, by 'Jinty' No 7316 working flat out. Thankfully, there appears to be no sign of a laundry basket on the platform! *28 May 1949*

155 Signalman Joe Crouchen waves a cheery greeting to the crews of class 2P No 40569, and BR class 9F No 92204, coasting down the bank through Midsomer Norton with the up 'Pines Express'. On the down line, a 'Jinty' 0-6-0T has paused from her shunting duties. *8 July 1960*

156 One event I always regret not having witnessed was the temporary loan of Johnson 0-4-4T No 58072 from Highbridge, to cover for a shortage of motive power at Bath during late April/early May 1955. Thankfully, Ivo photographed 'the old lady' many times during her brief sojourn on the main line, where she was employed on the evening local from Bath to Binegar and back. Here, she pauses at Midsomer Norton on the outward leg of the journey – the 6.05pm from Bath Green Park. *4 May 1955*

CHILCOMPTON TUNNEL

157 A 9F shows her worth – No 92204, with twelve on, climbs the long, hard slog at 1 in 53 from Midsomer Norton up to Chilcompton Tunnel with the 10.20am (SO) Liverpool – Bournemouth West. On a lovely hot Summer afternoon, there is little visual evidence to show how hard the engine was working, but Ivo said that the sound reverberating around the deep cutting leading up to the tunnel had been most impressive. *2 July 1960*

158 S & D class 7F No 53810 climbs out of the 66 yard long Chilcompton Tunnel with the 11.00am down freight from Bath. *11 August 1962*

CLIMBING TOWARDS CHILCOMPTON

159 The classic S&D locomotive combination. Ex-MR class 2P 4-4-0 No 509 pilots Stanier 'Black Five' 4-6-0 No 44830 with the down 'Pines Express'. The towering exhausts indicate that both engines are working close to 'all out' on the climb towards Chilcompton. *20 August 1949*

160 A pair of 2P's working in double-harness was once a familiar sight on the S&D, but in the post-war era this was no longer an everyday occurence. Nos 40698 and 40601 climb towards the rock cutting at Chilcompton with the very popular 'Trains Illustrated' excursion, run by the Ian Allan organisation. Earlier, the excursion had worked northbound over the S&D behind a SR 'Schools' class 4-4-0, assisted by No 40601. *25 April 1954*

161 Class 2P No 40564 and 4F No 44355 approach Binegar with the down 'Pines', passing S&D 7F No 13806. The latter was working down to Evercreech Junction with a brake van to bring a freight back to Bath. At Binegar, the 7F had been halted and shunted clear, so as not to check the progress of the S&D's 'premier' train. *2 August 1949*

BINEGAR

162 'Bulldog' class 3F 0-6-0 No 43248 has just returned to the S&D following an overhaul and, resplendent in British Railways unlined black livery, sets off with a down local comprising a rake of ex-L&SWR coaches. *20 August 1949*

BULLEID SUPERPOWER

163 The occasional use of two Bulleid Pacifics, in double-harness, on the 'Pines Express', was usually an indication of an unbalanced working. On a very blustery afternoon, No 34110 *66 Squadron* pilots No 34040 *Crewkerne* with the down 'Pines' on the climb southwards past Binegar Bottom, on the final stage of the long climb to the summit of the climb near Masbury.

'Battle of Britain' class No 34110, was the last of the Bulleid Pacifics to be constructed. Outshopped early in 1951, she entered service about the same time as the introduction of the first of the BR 'Standard' Pacifics No 70000 *Britannia*.

10 October 1953

MASBURY SUMMIT

164 The summit of the 7½ mile climb from Radstock was located 350 feet south of Bridge 69 – seen in the background of Ivo's photograph. Class 4F No 44146 pilots 'Black Five' No 45186 over the short level section at the summit – which extended for just 110 feet – with a south-bound express. *3 September 1949*

MASBURY

165 On a Sunday during February 1954, the Western Region ran two special test freight trains from Bath to Evercreech Junction and back, to reassess the haulage and braking power of the S&D class 7F locomotives. The second of these test trains – made up to equal 42 13-ton wagons – was hauled by big-boilered 7F, No 53807, and is seen storming up through Masbury with the return train. 'Jinty' class 3F 0-6-0T No 47557, working bunker-first, can just be discerned providing rear-end assistance. *14 February 1954*

WINSOR HILL — NORTH END

166 Another powerful combination – The up 'Pines Express', hauled by Stanier 'Black Five' No 44839 and Bulleid Pacific No 34044 *Woolacombe*, emerges from the north end of Winsor Hill Tunnel. By the early 1950's, the signalbox at Winsor Hill had been closed and the signals removed. But the cross-over between the up and down running lines, and the siding points leading into the stone quarries on the down side, had yet to be recovered. *12 April 1952*

167 No 53800, the doyenne of the S&D class 7F 2-8-0's, approaches Shepton Mallet with the 2.45pm (SO) Bournemouth West – Bristol, Temple Meads. Note that the engine carries the standard BR headlamp code, rather than the unique S&D code. When the Western Region gained control of the S&D in 1958, orders were issued that the S&D headcodes should no longer be used. However, this directive was soon to be overlooked with the S&D's own code again being displayed in deference to the wishes of 'the Western'! *16 August 1958*

SHEPTON MALLET

168 No 53802 climbs away southwards from Shepton Mallet with a down freight, passing under Bridge 87, which carried the GW branch from Witham to Wells and Yatton, and which features in Part 7 (see picture 242). After a short, but sharp, climb away from Shepton Mallet, the S&D line recommenced the long southbound descent of the Mendips, towards Evercreech Junction. *5 May 1951*

169 A 'Hall' class 4-6-0 sets off from Bath with an eastbound local passing, in the middle road, No 5094 *Tretower Castle;* the latter engine in ex-works condition following a recent overhaul and repaint at Swindon. *1 October 1949*

PART 5　BATH TO CHIPPENHAM (GWR)

170 Following an overhaul at Swindon, which included the fitting of a twin blastpipe and double chimney, No 6009 *King Charles II* approaches Bath Spa on the evening running-in turn with the 5.00pm Swindon to Bristol local.
30 May 1956

171 The high retaining wall on the east side of the line provides a 'bird's eye view' of No 7027 *Thornbury Castle* getting back into full stride with an up train which has called at Bath station. The engine was only a few months old when Ivo took this photograph in 1949.

SYDNEY GARDENS, BATH

The eastern exit of the Great Western line from Bath included the passage through Sydney Gardens – a wonderful location for 'watching the trains pass by', and little changed by the passage of time since the line between Chippenham and Bath was first opened to traffic on 30 June 1841.

172 With the regulator all but closed, No 4098 *Kidwelly Castle* glides majestically through Sydney Gardens with a down train, passing under the ornate iron footbridge designed by Isambard Kingdom Brunel.

14 May 1950

173 An unidentified *Hall* heads towards Bath with the Locomotive Club of Great Britain 'East Devon Rail Tour', passing a 'Hymek' diesel-hauled engineers' train held in the down loop. *2 May 1965*

WEST OF BATHAMPTON

Two miles east of Bath, on the approach to Bathampton station, the main line was flanked on both sides by a goods loop. Such was the volume of freight traffic, even in the latter days of steam, that almost invariably, one would find a heavy coal or freight train held in one of the loops waiting for a sufficient headway in the passenger traffic to run out and occupy the main line as far as the next loop or refuge.

174 Churchward 2-8-0, No 3864, takes on water whilst waiting in the up loop for the road to Westbury. This heavy goods train included coal traffic for the Southern Region. *21 August 1964*

175 The ex-Great Western 4-4-0 *City of Truro* coasts into Bathampton station. This famous old engine is seen here on a running-in turn, having just emerged from the Works at Swindon, where she had been overhauled and restored to traffic after many years of retirement. I wonder if the lineside would appear quite so deserted if *City of Truro* were to pass by in the 1980's? *25 March 1957*

BATHAMPTON

176 2-6-0, No 6378, has run down the main line to Bathampton wrong line with a west-bound Sunday excursion. The train is about to cross over to regain the down line to Bath. *21 May 1961*

177 No 6821 *Leaton Grange* runs down through Box station, some 2¾ miles east of Bathampton, with a Banbury to Bristol freight.

15 July 1964

BOX

178 No 7018 *Dryslļwyn Castle*, fitted with a self-weighing tender, speeds through Box on a special test run with the down 'Bristolian'. Ivo had received 'inside information' that the test run would be behind No 70018 (a 'Britannia' class locomotive) but it turned out to be a case of 'one too many noughts'! However, all must have been going well with No 7018 – as Ivo recorded the train being '3 minutes early' through Box.

6 May 1958

179 No 4920 *Dumbleton Hall* clears Middle Hill Tunnel and approaches Box station with a down freight. The old cast iron signs which proclaim that 'PASSENGERS are requested to CROSS the LINE by the BRIDGE', contrast with the modern, flimsy '6 car' plate which has been fixed to the gas standard on the left. Hopefully *Dumbleton Hall* will soon be seen again, following restoration at Buckfastleigh, on the Dart Valley Railway.
24 July 1964

180 During the latter part of the summer service in 1964, a steam-hauled train ran, on Saturdays only, between Calne and Weston Super Mare. Ivo captured BR 2-6-2T No 82001 in charge of this service – the 1.10pm (SO) from Calne – emerging from Middle Hill Tunnel.
5 September 1964

MIDDLE HILL TUNNEL

Both portals to Middle Hill Tunnel – just to the east of Box station – were most impressive and of considerable height, although once inside the tunnel, the dimensions reduce to no more than the general clearance.

BOX TUNNEL

Box Tunnel, planned by Brunel, is nearly two miles long and dead straight from end to end. There is a popular and long-standing legend that the rising sun may be seen shining right through the tunnel on just one day in the year, 9 April, Brunel's birthday. Disappointingly, this is not so, and it is perhaps worth repeating from his book. *Railway Elegance – Western Region Trains in the English Countryside*, Ivo's own words – 'Standing at the western end it is possible – if the weather is kind – to see the sun shine straight through the tunnel on just three days of the year, but the dates are 15-17 April; and because of the rising gradients of 1 in 100, the time is about half an hour after sunrise'.

181 No 6879 *Overton Grange* drifts out of the tunnel and past the Box down distant signal with a freight train bound for Bristol. *13 June 1964*

182 No 7029 *Clun Castle* emerges at speed with a Locomotive Club of Great Britain special. Notice how, since taking the photograph above, the arm of the Box down distant signal has been removed. *6 February 1965*

THINGLEY JUNCTION

183 Ivo has used artist's licence to include this photograph under the banner of 'Bath to Chippenham', in that GW Mogul No 6346 has just left the main line at Thingley Junction, two miles west of Chippenham, and is heading southwards towards Melksham and Westbury. The main line can, however, be seen in the background to Ivo's photograph. *16 March 1963*

CHIPPENHAM

184 SR rebuilt pacific No 34017 *Ilfracombe* passes Chippenham at speed on 27 April 1963 with a special from Southampton. On the same day Southampton played Manchester United in the semi-final of the FA cup at Villa Park, Birmingham. Was this, perhaps, one of the many special trains run in conjunction with that event?

185 Heading a Bristol-bound train, No 6955 *Lyndcott Hall* has reduced speed to negotiate the severe curved approach to the junction with the main line at Bathampton. On the up side of the line, notice how the siting of the starting signals necessitated the use of centrally pivoted signal arms. *20 May 1950*

PART 6
BATHAMPTON TO WESTBURY (GWR)

At Bathampton, 2 miles east of Bath, the line to Trowbridge and Westbury branches away from the Bath to Paddington main line. Following the opening of the Severn Tunnel in 1886, and the connection with the London & South Western Railway at Salisbury, the Bathampton to Westbury line became part of an important cross-country route, linking South Wales and Bristol with the South Coast.

186 Having been held for some time in the up loop just west of Bathampton station, 0-6-0PT No 3739 sets off with a goods train bound for Westbury. *20 August 1964*

BATHAMPTON – THE OLD & NEW SIGNALBOXES

187 No 5022 *Wigmore Castle* slows to call at Bathampton with the 5.00pm down local from Swindon to Bristol – another service regularly used for running-in engines following overhaul at Swindon. The train is passing the old signalbox, which until 1956, controlled the junction with the line to Trowbridge and Westbury. *9 May 1953*

188 In 1956, a new signalbox, sited on the up side of the main line, was brought into use. 'Castle' class No 5081 *Lockheed Hudson* eases the 5.35pm Salisbury to Cardiff train over the junction points. *7 May 1963*

FRESHFORD

From Bathampton, the line threads the very beautiful Limpley Stoke valley along which, for some miles, the railway, river, road and canal keep company – the Kennet & Avon Canal crossing and recrossing both the railway and the river on handsome aqueducts. After passing through Limpley Stoke the railway served the delightful village of Freshford and, happily, is still doing so today.

189 The 9.10am (Sundays only) Cardiff to Portsmouth train approaches Freshford, passing the signalbox at the eastern end of the goods loops and sidings originally laid down to serve coal traffic from the Limpley Stoke to Camerton branch. (see Part 8)
5 March 1961

190 Rebuilt Bulleid Pacific, No 34042 *Dorchester* passes through the station with a Sunday excursion from the Southern Region.
5 March 1961

Freshford signalbox was severely damaged in the early 1950's, when the driver of a heavy goods train, held in the up loop, misread the main line signal for that of the goods line. Opening the regulator, his engine promptly ran through the trap points and into the box! The 'making good' to the brickwork can be seen at the near corner of the signalbox in the lower picture.

191 BR class 5 No 73001 emerges from 'The Avenue' with the 7.35am (SO) Nottingham to Bournemouth, a service which, until 1962, had run via the Somerset & Dorset line each summer. The siding, by this date little used, on the far side of the main line served as a goods refuge, and was known as 'Cocklebury Siding'.   *29 August 1964*

192 No 7829 *Ramsbury Manor* heads away westwards from Bradford on Avon and towards 'The Avenue' with the 8.48am (SO) train from New Milton to Swansea – a service which ran via Bournemouth, Poole, Wimborne and Salisbury. Hence, it was not renowned as being the fastest of trains!   *29 August 1964*

NEAR BRADFORD ON AVON

Beyond Freshford, the valley narrows and from Avoncliff the railway, river and canal again run a parallel course. On the eastern approach to the picturesque Wiltshire town of Bradford on Avon, the railway is bounded on both sides by a row of tall trees – a location known locally as 'The Avenue'. It is also a place of special significance for me; – it was here that I first recollect the sight of a steam locomotive.

193 No 6849 *Walton Grange* bursts out of the tunnel east of Bradford station with a Sunday parcels train, and passes the diminutive Greenland Mill Crossing box before heading towards the junction with the Thingley to Westbury line at Bradford Junction. *16 April 1961*

194 No 6029 *King Edward VIII* passes over the River Avon at Greenland Mill Crossing, with a diverted Sunday morning express. The sight of a 'King' at this location was a *very* rare occurrence; the class was permitted to run over the line only in cases of emergency, and subject to an overall speed limit of 30mph. *16 April 1961*

BRADFORD ON AVON – GREENLAND MILL CROSSING

Immediately to the east of Bradford tunnel, the railway crosses, on the level, a lane leading from the town centre to Greenland Mill.

BRADFORD JUNCTION SIGNALBOX

195 East of Bradford on Avon, the branch from Bathampton joins the line from Thingley Junction, near Chippenham, to Westbury. The line from Thingley divides to form a triangular junction, with one connection – the original main line – heading towards Trowbridge and Westbury, and the other curving round towards Bradford.

Signalman Mervyn Halbrook on duty in the signalbox at Bradford Junction. At the time of writing (June 1987), the box survives complete with semaphore signals. A vestige of the steam age, the box is linked to the modern 'panel' installations at Swindon, Bristol and Westbury. It is scheduled for early closure – the last ex-GW box in use in Wiltshire.

MELKSHAM

North from Bradford Junction, the line to Thingley passes through Holt, the junction of a single line from Patney and Chirton, before reaching Melksham.

196 BR Class 9F No 92220 *Evening Star* runs through the once-busy station at Melksham with a Banbury to Westbury freight.
17 October 1964

197 No 6829 *Burmington Grange* sets off with a West-bury to Bristol, Temple Meads stopping train. In the background, beyond the water tower, is the old engine shed, brought into use in 1875. However, most of the allocation of locomotives transferred to the new depot opened at nearby Westbury in April 1915. Thereafter, the locomotive facilities at the Trowbridge were run down, the shed finally closing on 2 June 1923.
From a colour transparency – courtesy M. S. Sims.

TROWBRIDGE

At the outset of preparing this book, I asked Ivo to consider one special favour – that he would include some photographs of Trowbridge – my 'home' station, which I cannot recall having previously featured in any similar publication. Ivo immediately agreed to my request – but then promptly added that as he had never taken a single photograph at Trowbridge he would, 'allocate' me two pages, but I would have to track down the appropriate pictures. Three months, and many abortive 'phone calls later, I began to wonder whether anyone had ever bothered to 'click the shutter' at Trowbridge station. Many friends offered me a fine selection of prints – covering just about every conceivable lineside location . . . except Trowbridge! Finally, close to the point of dispair, I was rescued by John Sparkes and Maurice Sims, to whom I acknowledge my grateful thanks.

The railway at Trowbridge, as I best remember it, during the 1950's and early 1960's was still very busy and outwardly little changed from former 'Great Western' days. In addition to the cross-country passenger and freight traffic between South Wales, Bristol and even Wolverhampton, to and from Weymouth, Portsmouth and Brighton, there existed a variety of local services. Trowbridge could even boast a direct service to and from Paddington, trains departing from 'the bay' (platform 3) and running via Holt Junction and Devizes to join the 'Berks & Hants' main line at Patney and Chirton.

198 No 5039 *Rhuddlan Castle* prepares to leave from platform 2 with the 3.15pm train from Westbury to Reading, which ran via Holt Junction and the Devizes branch. The bay platform (No 3) is just out of camera, to the right. Courtesy J. H. Sparkes.
7 May 1964

199 On a wet morning, BR class 4 2-6-0 No 76041 enters the station on a running-in turn from Swindon. The signal to the right – on the down platform – authorised various backing movements to be made, the appropriate route selected, being displayed on the indicator seen below the signal arm. There were extensive sidings on both sides of the line and a healthy goods traffic – as witnessed by the large covered goods shed seen behind No 76041. Trowbridge signal box is also just discernible in the left background. Courtesy J. H. Sparkes.   *14 April 1964*

200 No 6900 *Abney Hall* pulls away with a local bound for Westbury, and is about to pass under the road bridge at the down end of the station. Platforms 2 and 3 can be seen to the left. Although Trowbridge station remains open to traffic, all of the buildings seen in this view have been swept away and the platforms much reduced in length. New station buildings have been promised! From a colour transparency – courtesy M. S. Sims.

201 No 7907 *Hart Hall* passes Hawkeridge Junction in charge of a down freight heading towards Westbury.

10 October 1964

HAWKERIDGE JUNCTION

On the north-east approach to Westbury from Trowbridge, a connecting line was laid down in 1942 to make an east-facing link with the West of England main line. The connection with the Trowbridge line was made at Hawkeridge, where a new signalbox also controlled the entrance to sidings serving a nearby supplies depot established by the War Department.

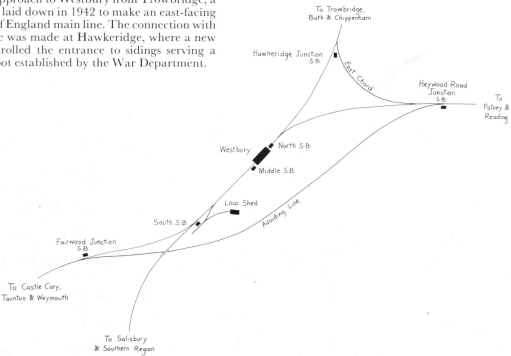

To Trowbridge, Bath & Chippenham

Hawkeridge Junction S.B.

East Chord

Heywood Road Junction S.B.

To Patney & Reading

Westbury   North S.B.

Middle S.B.

Loco Shed

South S.B.

Avoiding Line

Fairwood Junction S.B.

To Castle Cary, Taunton & Weymouth

To Salisbury & Southern Region

202 Ex-LMS Stanier 2-6-0 No 42954, running in after a general overhaul at Swindon, approaches Westbury in the early morning with a pick-up goods. The connecting line curving away towards Heywood Road Junction, was originally laid down to create a war-time diversionary route between Bristol and London, and so avoid reversal at Westbury.

17 October 1965

203 The construction of the war-time link – which became known as the 'East Chord' – created a triangular layout of lines which was sometimes used to turn locomotives (and could be so used for steam-hauled specials today!). Ivo photographed Bulleid Pacific No 35019 *French Line CGT* using the East Chord to turn before heading home to Salisbury. Earlier in the day, No 35019 had worked a perishables train up from Weymouth. In the background is the well-known landmark – the Westbury white horse cut into the hillside near Bratton.

7 August 1965

204 An unidentified 'Hall' running into Westbury from the Trowbridge direction with the 12.50pm Cardiff to Brighton. In the middle-distance the station pilot, an 0-6-0PT, waits on the Patney line, built by the GWR and opened in 1900 as part of the new direct route from Paddington to the West of England, of which the final link between Castle Cary and Cogload, near Taunton, was opened in 1906.

11 May 1963

WESTBURY ARRIVALS & DEPARTURES

205 No 6999 *Capel Dewi Hall* sets off past Hawkeridge Junction towards Trowbridge with a banana special. This route, the 14 mile section from Thingley Junction, was the first line to reach Westbury, and was opened on 5 September 1848. *10 October 1964*

206 BR class 5 No 73080 leaves platform 4 with a local – the starting signal is *off* for the Trowbridge line, whilst the distant arm underneath is worked by Hawkeridge Junction and 'slotted' from Westbury North box, seen to the far left. *10 October 1964*

207 Stanier 'Black Five' No 45434 shunting some pigeon vans at the north end of the station which, until 1984, sported an impressive array of semaphores – including a large gantry hidden from view by the road bridge spanning the lines beyond Westbury North signal-box. *28 August 1965*

WESTBURY STATION – NORTH END

On completion of the direct route from London to the West of England in 1906, Westbury became an important railway centre forming the 'crossroads' with the line from South Wales and Bristol to the South Coast. Early in 1933, however, the station lost some of its through trains, following the opening of the Westbury 'avoiding' line between Heywood Road and Fairwood junctions.

208 4-6-0 No 45434 has now remarshalled her train of pigeon vans and prepares to set off past the 'Middle' signalbox.　　*28 August 1965*

WESTBURY STATION – SOUTH END

209 A pair of passing strangers – Longmoor Military Railway 0-6-0ST No 196, and BR 'U.S.A.' 0-6-0T No 30064, returning from display at an 'Open Day' held at Bath Road depot, Bristol. A pause was made for water at Westbury, before running on to Salisbury, where the two engines parted company to regain their respective home territories.　　*25 October 1966*

210 Yet more of Westbury's once impressive range of semaphore signals – SR Pacific No 34019 *Bideford* is backing down to take over a Southern Counties Touring Society special to the West Country. The train had been brought down from London by BR class 5 No 73065, seen to the left of the Bulleid Pacific.

13 November 1966

211 No 73065 features again – but this picture is included to show yet another of Westbury's signalboxes – the 'South' box which controlled the junction between the West of England and Salisbury lines, as well as access from the down yard and the motive power depot, which lay beyond the rear of the box. *13 November 1966*

WESTBURY MOTIVE POWER DEPOT

213 The turntable with LMS class 8F No 48415 in the process of being turned. *10 May 1959*

214 The coaling stage with 2-6-2T No 5542 receiving attention. *10 May 1959*

212 A general panoramic view taken in 1959, when Westbury Shed (code 82D) still retained an allocation of around 80 locomotives which included three examples of the 56XX/66XX class – one of which figures in the left foreground – which were used primarily for banking duties between Westbury and Upton Scudamore, on the line towards Salisbury. *10 May 1959*

215 SR class U 2-6-0 No 31632 on shed prior to working back to Salisbury. *1 November 1964*

216 GW 'Hall' class 4-6-0's No 6990 *Witherslack Hall* and No 6908 *Downham Hall* stand alongside 2-8-0 No 3864, outside the 4-road running shed. *20 September 1964*

217 The view from the south end of Westbury station – and the main item of interest must be the eight-wheel tender attached to No 6951 *Impney Hall*. Contrary to popular belief, this was *not* the tender from *The Great Bear*, but a special experimental tender built by the GWR in 1931.

16 September 1956

PART 7
WESTBURY TO UPTON SCUDAMORE
and
WESTBURY – WITHAM – WELLS (GWR)

218 South-east of Westbury station, the line to Salisbury parts company with the main, West of England line, to climb for more than two miles, past Dilton Marsh Halt, to the summit at Upton Scudamore. 'Castle' class No 5087 *Tintern Abbey* assists an unidentified 'Hall' up the bank with the 12.50pm Cardiff to Brighton train. *7 May 1960*

219 No 5911 *Preston Hall*, assisted by a 2-6-2 tank, heads southwards towards Warminster with the 12.50pm Cardiff to Brighton.

On 2 April 1950, the operating responsibility for the old GW line from Westbury (exclusive) to Salisbury passed to the Southern Region of BR, following a revision of the regional boundaries. Hence the appearance, in some of Ivo's photographs, of upper quadrant semaphore signals at Upton Scudamore.

7 June 1960

UPTON SCUDAMORE BANK

220 BR class 9F 2-10-0 No 92157 vigorously climbing the bank with a train of empty oil tanks returning to Fawley, near Southampton. After only a few months, this traffic was diverted away from the Westbury route.

28 April 1962

UPTON SCUDAMORE BANK – THE SUMMIT

221 SR class S15 4-6-0 No 30827 makes a cautious descent of the bank with a banana special. At Westbury the train would be handed over to a WR engine. The summit of the bank occurred immediately beyond the overbridge in the background.

7 June 1960

222 No 5014 *Goodrich Castle* tops the bank in fine style, heading the 'Docks Express', an Ian Allan 'Trains Illustrated' excursion. Most of the freight traffic bound for Salisbury and the SR required rear-end assistance between Westbury and Upton Scudamore. The short siding seen here served as a refuge for those occasions when the signalman at Upton Scudamore was unable to permit a bank engine clearance to cross over onto the up line and return immediately to Westbury.

16 September 1956

EASTERN
INVASION

223 Class A3 Pacific No 4472 *Flying Scotsman* heads a Warwickshire Railway Society excursion, passing the Upton Scudamore down distant signal on the climb towards the summit of the bank.

17 August 1964

224 Class A2 Pacific No 60532 *Blue Peter* running 'light engine' towards Salisbury. Earlier *Blue Peter* had hauled a Locomotive Club of Great Britain special from Waterloo to Exeter and on to Westbury. Here the train was taken over by BR 'Britannia' class No 70004 for the return, via Salisbury, to Waterloo.

14 August 1966

FAIRWOOD JUNCTION

From Westbury South Junction, where the Salisbury line diverged, the main line to Weymouth and the West of England turned westwards to run just over a mile to Fairwood, where a junction was formed with the Westbury avoiding line.

225 Stanier class 5 No 44691 takes the line into Westbury, at Fairwood Junction, with the 11.05am (SO) Weymouth to Wolverhampton. In the foreground is the avoiding line which by-passed Westbury station and rejoined the original main line to London at Heywood Road Junction. *26 June 1965*

226 An 0-6-0PT heads east with a short stone train, past the water tank which provided the supplies to the Fairwood troughs. This is another picture of special significance, reminding me of my last (unofficial!) footplate trip on BR, on an 0-6-0PT from Radstock and Frome to Westbury in 1964. *9 May 1964*

227 SR Pacific No 35026 *Lamport & Holt Line* comes out from Westbury and across the junction with one of the many 'specials' which ran during the latter months of 1966.

15 October 1966

228 One of the best remembered of the Ian Allan railtours must be the 'Railway World' excursion of 9 May 1964, run to commemorate the sixtieth anniversary of *City of Truro*'s exploits on the Wellington bank in 1904. High speed runs were planned between London and Plymouth, outward via Westbury, and returning by the original Bristol route. No 4079 *Pendennis Castle*, allocated to the London to Plymouth leg had to be halted near Lavington and removed from the train at Westbury. Here No 6999 'Capel Dewi Hall', the only available engine, was commandeered to take the train on to Taunton where another 'Castle' was held in reserve.

No 6999 is seen here setting off in very determined style from Westbury, passing over the water troughs just west of Fairwood Junction.

9 May 1964

229 No 6956 *Mottram Hall* comes out from Frome and rejoins the main line at Clink Road Junction with a Weymouth to Bristol train. The cut-off line is seen running south-westwards towards Blatchbridge. *27 September 1952*

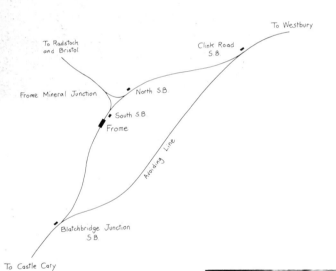

CLINK ROAD JUNCTION

As at Westbury, the GWR constructed an avoiding line at Frome. Opened in 1933, the cut-off extended from Clink Road Junction in the east to Blatchbridge Junction in the west, a distance of 2 miles 57 yards.

230 Twenty years earlier, during the summer of 1931, Ivo – then at college – had heard rumours that a new railway line was being constructed near Frome. On a Sunday afternoon, Ivo persuaded his father to take him for a car ride and 'discovered' the building of the cut-off line. The work was being undertaken by the firm of Logan and Hemingway, and amongst the stud of locomotives employed, were these two 0-6-0 saddle tanks, numbered 8 and 3, and built by Manning, Wardle and Company.

231 An 'Ian Allan' excursion, westbound hauled by SR 'Battle of Britain' Pacific No 34050 *Royal Observer Corps*. (A special pet of Ivo's as he was a member of the Royal Observer Corps for twenty-five years.) *22 September 1962*

232 No 6908 *Downham Hall* heads a class 'H' eastbound freight, which had been routed along the cut-off line, past the signalbox at Clink Road. *22 September 1962*

233 The 11.10am (SO) Wolverhampton to Weymouth is in the charge of No 6851 *Hurst Grange* travelling westward from Blatchbridge. *29 August 1964*

BLATCHBRIDGE JUNCTION
South of Frome the avoiding line rejoins the original route to Castle Cary and the West at Blatchbridge Junction.

234 Having been stripped of name and numberplates, *Bucklebury Grange* is still identifiable by the number, 6803, hurriedly painted onto the buffer beam and cabside. Seen here in charge of the 11.05am (SO) Weymouth to Wolverhampton, she eases over the junction at Blatchbridge before slowing for the scheduled call at Frome. *10 July 1965*

235 Ex-GW 4-6-0 No 6955 *Lydcott Hall* nearing Witham with the 5.50pm (SO) Weymouth to Westbury.

7 July 1962

WITHAM

Here a branch left the main line to run, via Shepton Mallet and Wells, to Yatton on the original West of England main line from Bristol. The branch was known as the Cheddar Valley Line or, often, as the 'Strawberry Line', a reference to the special traffic once carried to markets throughout the country.

236 A pair of 2-6-2 tanks, Nos 4103 and 6148, run onto the main line at Witham, having traversed the Cheddar Valley line from Yatton with the 'Mendip Rail Tour' organised by the Home Counties Railway Society.

6 October 1963

237 The epitome of the branch line freight train; pannier tank No 4607 ambles away from Cranmore with a pick-up goods bound for Frome.
7 August 1962

CRANMORE

3¾ miles west of Witham, the now truncated branch line connects with the private rail system of Foster Yeoman which serves the company's vast quarry complex at Merehead. Two miles further west, Cranmore station is reached, now well-known as the headquarters of the East Somerset Railway, established under the leadership of the renowned railway and wild-life artist, David Shepherd.

238 BR class 3 2-6-2T No 82039, arriving at Cranmore with the 3.28pm train from Witham to Yatton and Bristol, Temple Meads. *3 November 1962*

239 In pouring rain, 0-6-0PT No 9754 is busy shunting bitumen tank wagons at Cranmore, a traffic which for many years, frustrated the wishes of the East Somerset Railway to gain rail access into Cranmore station.

30 May 1964

240 The last day of passenger traffic on the Cheddar Valley line. Collett 0-6-0 No 3218, prepares to leave Cranmore with the very last train from Witham. Both the station and signalbox have been saved and superbly restored, as I witnessed when filming sequences for the BBC television documentary *Return to Evercreech Junction*.

7 September 1963

BETWEEN CRANMORE
AND SHEPTON MALLET

241 No 4607, with the branch freight, nears the end of the climb from Shepton Mallet, and runs towards Cranmore. This is close to the location which now forms the western limit of the preserved East Somerset Railway.

7 August 1962

242 BR class 3 No 82036, sweeps down the bank towards Shepton Mallet and is about to pass over the Somerset & Dorset line (see picture 168) with a Witham to Wells train.

28 July 1962

The Great Western station at Shepton was known as 'High Street' and, as the title suggests, was conveniently close to the town centre. Both views show 0-6-0 No 3218 working the last eastbound train, the 2.45pm Yatton to Witham on the final day of passenger traffic.

An interesting detail often missed by modellers – notice how the station siding crosses over the down loop and connects to the up line, thereby conforming to the preferred practice of avoiding, wherever possible, the provision of a facing connection to a running line. *7 September 1963*

SHEPTON MALLET GREAT WESTERN

245 No 3218 again, running in with the final passenger train from Yatton to Witham. The fireman prepares to hand over the single-line token to the Wells signalman.

7 September 1963

WELLS

Wells 'Tucker Street' station was one of those locations where, for operating purposes, down trains (from Yatton) suddenly become UP trains when proceeding onwards in the same direction (towards Witham)! Similar confusion, of course, ruled in the opposite direction.

246 Earlier the same day, Ivatt 2-6-2T No 41245, after arrival with the 1.45pm (SO) from Yatton, which terminated at Wells to form a return working to Yatton.

It is interesting to compare the marked lack of 'last day supporters' with the scenes witnessed only a few years later – in particular, perhaps, the closure of the nearby Somerset & Dorset line early in 1966. *7 September 1963*

NEAR WELLS

247 The 'Mendip Rail Tour', with 2-6-2 tanks Nos 4103 and 6148, near Wells with the 'special' from Bristol which ran along the line from Yatton to Witham.

6 October 1963

248 Two ex-GW 0-6-0's, Nos 3218 and 2251, stand outside the small motive power shed at Wells during the final week prior to closure of this shed.

4 September 1963

WELLS SHED

FROME

After many years of neglect, during which period the Brunel overall roof was allowed to fall into disrepair, this fine feature has now been restored, albeit to span only a single set of rails.

249 On a gloomy autumn afternoon Ivatt 2-6-2T No 41245 is about to leave with a local for the Witham-Yatton line. On the left 0-6-0PT No 9612 bereft of smokebox numberplate, rests before running down the branch to Radstock.   *20 October 1962*

PART 8
FROME TO PENSFORD
and
THE CAMERTON BRANCH (GWR)

The North Somerset branch from Frome to Bristol, was planned and built in two separate parts – the Frome to Radstock line and, later, the Bristol to Radstock section. Passenger traffic over the line was withdrawn on 2nd November 1959, the last trains running on the preceding Saturday

250 Stanier Class 5 4-6-0 No 44691 arriving at Frome with the 10.45am (SO) Wolverhampton-Weymouth.
14 August 1965

WHATLEY QUARRY STONE TRAINS

2 ½ miles west of Frome, the North Somerset branch serves a private line which runs to the large stone quarry at Whatley.

251 0-6-0PT No 4673 with a train of empties from Frome for the Whatley Quarry, heads towards the exchange sidings at Hapsford.
31 March 1965

252 No 4673 nearing Frome with a loaded train of stone.
24 October 1964

253 Sentinel No 1 shunting wagons in the exchange sidings at Hapsford. This was one of the four vertical boiler, geared, Sentinels used on the privately-owned quarry line.   *8 March 1968*

THE WHATLEY QUARRY LINE

The large stone quarry at Whatley, near Frome, was originally connected to the ex-GW North Somerset branch by a narrow gauge line. During the Second World War the privately-owned line was converted to standard gauge and when Ivo first visited the line in the 1950's, the motive power was provided in the form of four Sentinel steam engines together with a solitary 0-4-0 saddle tank. In the early 1970's the quarry line was extensively realigned, including the abandonment of the exchange sidings at Hapsford, and the provision of a new connection with the BR line ½ mile nearer to Radstock. The upgraded line could now be worked by main line BR diesels.

254 0-4-0ST *Medway* at Hapsford. Built by Andrew Barclay in 1903, she was sent for scrap in 1956. The somewhat squat appearance, with a cut-down cab, was necessary to clear the very limited headroom under a road-bridge on the line to Whatley.
22 October 1955

255 Sentinel No 2 about to enter the short tunnel under the Frome to Mells road at the sinisterly-titled 'Murder Combe'. *24 May 1958*

256 Sentinel No 2 is seen again, passing through the woods on the severely curved approach to the quarry at Whatley. *8 September 1956*

MELLS ROAD   **257** 0-6-0PT No 3746, with a pick-up goods, sets off from Mells Road Station, 5¼ miles west of Frome – and some 2 miles across the fields from the village of Mells! A siding in the small goods yard served as a connection with another private line leading to the quarries at Vobster.
31 March 1964

258 2-6-2T No 4572, and 0-6-0PT No 3746, pull away from Radstock with a solitary brake van in tow. Unlike the remainder of the North Somerset line, the 3 mile section between Mells Road and Radstock was laid to double track.
15 August 1954

**RADSTOCK
(GWR)**

259 Driver Herbie Loader kindly halts his little Peckett 0-4-0ST for Ivo to photograph. Note the broken buffer head and, on the running plate, the bunch of catkins picked from a lineside bush!
29 April 1966

260 The Peckett busily engaged in shunting duties at Kilmersdon. *29 April 1966*

KILMERSDON COLLIERY

The north Somerset coalfield was centred upon the town of Radstock, and Kilmersdon – one of the once numerous collieries – was brought into production in 1878. Kilmersdon Colliery was linked to the GW railway by means of a standard gauge branch, which included a self-acting incline. Initially the private line connecting the colliery yard with the head of the incline was worked by horses, but subsequently steam power was introduced. In September 1929, the original locomotive was replaced by a small 0-4-0ST, supplied by Peckett & Company of Bristol. This little engine was to remain working at Kilmersdon until closure of the pit in 1973

HALLATROW

In 1882 Hallatrow became the junction from a branch line to Camerton which, in 1910, was extended along the Cam valley to Limpley Stoke. In 1932, however, the original section between Hallatrow and Camerton was closed and the single line lifted. The truncated Limpley Stoke-Camerton branch is featured at the end of this section.

261 BR Class 3 2-6-2T No 82007 pulls away from the picturesque station at Hallatrow with a Sunday train from Bristol to Frome, during the final year of passenger traffic over the North Somerset line. *12 July 1959*

262 Ex-GW 2-6-2T No 4103 pauses by the water column with the 5.00pm coal train from Radstock to East Depot at Bristol. The station footbridge, with its open-latticed sides and corrugated-iron roof, is worthy of close attention by the modeller of the GWR. *28 April 1964*

263 The Hallatrow signalman prepares to collect the single-line token from the driver of 2-6-2T No 6148, arriving with the 5.00pm coal train from Radstock. No 4103 is waiting for line clearance with the late-running 2.40pm goods from Bristol to Frome.

26 March 1961

264 No 6148 passes the signalbox with a coal train from Old Mills Colliery. The box, which contained a locking frame of 67 levers, including 12 'spares', was erected in 1909 in conjunction with the building of the Camerton-Limpley Stoke Railway. At the same time the station was enlarged including the provision of a second platform, this allowing passenger trains to 'cross' one another.

31 March 1964

265 No 6148 approaches Clutton from Hallatrow, passing the up fixed distant signal with the 5.00pm coal train from Radstock. *27 September 1963*

266 No 6148 climbing away from Clutton, again with the 5.00pm from Radstock. *13 April 1964*

267 Climbing between Pensford and Clutton, No 6148 and brake van forming the 2.05pm from Bristol East Depot to work the 3.44pm coal train from Old Mills Colliery.

14 April 1964

268 Descending cautiously towards Pensford, No 6148 passes the Clutton down distant signal with a heavy coal train from Radstock.

10 April 1964

CLUTTON
WOODS

PENSFORD VIADUCT

269 The most impressive structure on the North Somerset line – Pensford viaduct was located immediately to the south of the station and dominated the village. 2-6-2T No 4103 crosses the viaduct with the 2.40pm goods from Bristol East Depot.

26 March 1964

270 A pannier tank and brake van, forming the 2.40pm Bristol to Old Mills, slips through the countryside near Chelwood.

26 September 1963

NEAR CHELWOOD

RUNNING DOWNHILL NEAR CHELWOOD

271 An ex-GW 0-6-0PT runs downhill through delightful countryside towards Chelwood, between Clutton and Pensford, with a coal train from Old Mills Colliery. *26 September 1963*

CLIMBING TOWARDS WHITCHURCH

272 A final glimpse of the picturesque North Somerset line, with the ever faithful No 6148, climbing near Malrewood, towards Whitchurch, with another load of coal bound for the Portishead power station. *13 April 1964*

273 On the outward journey, No 9612 propelled her train towards Camerton. Here she has just passed under the S&D line at Midford, heading westwards towards Combe Hay.

THE LIMPLEY STOKE TO CAMERTON BRANCH

The Camerton branch joined with the GW Bathampton to Trowbridge and Westbury line just to the north of Limpley Stoke, and ran in a westerly direction through the very picturesque valleys of the Midford and Cam brooks. Passenger services survived only a few years, but the line remained open to freight traffic until 1951, although in the latter years, following closure of the last of the collieries in the Cam valley, the branch carried very little traffic.

The rails of the Camerton branch remained in situ until, towards the end of 1957, recovery of the track commenced at Camerton, working back towards Limpley Stoke. On Saturday, 15 February 1958, the demolition train, consisting of GW 0-6-0PT No 9612, together with a brake van, bolster wagon and two trucks, left Limpley Stoke at 8.00am heading towards Camerton. Ivo 'gave chase', photographing the train at many different locations on both the outward and return journeys.

A PAUSE IN THE CHASE

274 On the return run, Ivo has overtaken No 9612, and is able to pause and obtain this picture of the train between Dunkerton and Combe Hay. Ivo's Bentley stands ready for 'the off'!

NEARING
MONKTON COMBE

275 Running through the beautiful Midford valley, near Tucking Mill, between Midford and Monkton Combe.

JOINING THE MAIN LINE AT LIMPLEY STOKE

276 No 9612 rounds the curve to run the final ½ mile parallel to the main line, to which access was gained immediately north of Limpley Stoke station. Dundas aqueduct, which carries the Kennet & Avon Canal over both the river Avon and the line to Bathampton may just be discernible in the right background.

THE TITFIELD THUNDERBOLT

Undoubtedly the Limpley Stoke to Camerton line is best remembered by many people as the location chosen for the film *The Titfield Thunderbolt*. Made in 1952, after the line had closed to all traffic, the film has become one of the comedy 'classics' made by the famous Ealing Studios.

277 Star of the film – 0-4-2 *Lion*, built for the Liverpool & Manchester Railway in 1838 by Todd, Kitson and Laird – resting in the yard at Monkton Combe, after arriving on the branch at Westbury. *21 June 1952*

278 A few days later, the *Lion* had been temporarily rechristened *Thunderbolt*, and had gained some additional decoration to the tall chimney! Ivo photographed her standing beside the water tower erected by the film company between 'Titfield' (Monkton Combe) and Tucking Mill. The tower was, of course, merely a 'dummy'; water for the locomotive was obtained from Midford Brook – seen in the background – via a fire pump. *26 June 1952*

BETWEEN TAKES

279 Left: Approaching Midford with a well-filled guard's van! and . . . .

280 (Below) . . . . stationary, under Combe Hay Bridge, where the appearance of *Thunderbolt* has obviously aroused great enthusiasm amongst the local schoolchildren — many of whom were used as 'extras'.

281 A final glimpse of *Steam around Bath* – a Somerset & Dorset goods storms up the 1 in 50 grade out of Bath, and is about to disappear from view into Devonshire Tunnel.

When Ivo took this evocative picture, there was no reason to think that such an everyday sight would ever be any different. But not only was the S&D itself to 'disappear from view', but also several of the other lines portrayed in this book. Those which have survived the closure of country stations and the 'rationalisation' of the post-Beeching era, present today a very different railway scene to that captured through the lens of Ivo's camera.